Animal Kingdom

by Joshua BishopRoby

Science Contributor
Sally Ride Science
Science Consultants
Thomas R. Ciccone, Science Educator
Ronald Edwards, Ph.D., Science Educator

MISSION: SCIENCE

Developed with contributions from Sally Ride Science™

Sally Ride Science

Sally Ride Science™ is an innovative content company dedicated to fueling young people's interests in science.

Our publications and programs provide opportunities for students and teachers to explore the captivating world of science—from astrobiology to zoology.

We bring science to life and show young people that science is creative, collaborative, fascinating, and fun.

To learn more, visit www.SallyRideScience.com

First hardcover edition published in 2009 by
Compass Point Books
151 Good Counsel Drive
P.O. Box 669
Mankato, MN 56002-0669

Editor: Jennifer VanVoorst
Designer: Heidi Thompson
Editorial Contributor: Sue Vander Hook

Art Director: LuAnn Ascheman-Adams
Creative Director: Joe Ewest
Editorial Director: Nick Healy
Managing Editor: Catherine Neitge

 This book was manufactured with paper containing at least 10 percent post-consumer waste.

Library of Congress Cataloging-in-Publication Data
BishopRoby, Joshua.
  Animal kingdom / by Joshua BishopRoby.
  p. cm. — (Mission: Science)
  ISBN 978-0-7565-4057-9 (library binding)
1. Animals—Classification—Juvenile literature. I. Title. II. Series.
  QL351.B48 2009
  590—dc22   2008037574

Visit Compass Point Books on the Internet at *www.compasspointbooks.com*
or e-mail your request to *custserv@compasspointbooks.com*

Table of Contents

Fascinating Animals

Whether it's a cat or a dog, a cow or a frog, a lizard, a deer, or a whale, animals are fascinating. Bugs, fish, lobsters, earthworms, hawks, and many more—they are all members of the animal kingdom.

Animals are part of our everyday lives. Look out a window, and you will most likely see birds in the sky. Perhaps you have a pet dog or cat at home. Go outside and turn over a rock, and you might find a bug or a worm hiding underneath.

However, there are thousands of animals in the world that you don't see on a regular day. Some of them are very strange. There are fish that can flop over land from one pond to another and octopuses that can open jars with their

arms. Have you ever seen a platypus? It has fur like a cat, a bill like a duck, a tail like a beaver, and webbed feet like an otter. This mammal swims in rivers and lays eggs. The male platypus has a spur on its hind foot that can deliver painful venom to an unsuspecting visitor.

There's one type of animal, though, that you see every day—humans. You are a member of the animal kingdom, too. Although humans are very different from fish, octopuses, platypuses, and other creatures, humans do have a lot of things in common with other animals.

All of these organisms are members of the animal kingdom.

In a world with millions of different kinds of animals, scientists need a way to know which animal another scientist is talking about. Zoologists—scientists who study animals—use an organizing system called taxonomy to identify animals. Taxonomy organizes animals into groups based on how they are alike or different.

To understand taxonomy, imagine yourself as a salesperson at a large car dealership. There are many different cars—red cars, blue cars, white cars, trucks, vans, and convertibles. Some cars run on gas, while others use a combination of gas and electricity. How do you organize these very different vehicles?

You could start by dividing the lot into cars and trucks. Then you might put the cars into two groups: four-door cars and two-door cars. You could split the two-door cars into hardtops and convertibles. Then you could refer to the different convertibles by their manufacturers (Ford, Honda, Toyota, Chrysler, etc.). Then you could say, "The red Toyota convertible needs a tire fixed." If it started raining, you could say, "Get the convertibles inside!"

A zoologist examines a giant squid.

Zoologists use taxonomy in the same way. A zoologist might talk about an animal by using its scientific name: "*Felis silvestris* [house cats] make good pets." Or the zoologist might refer to a whole group of animals and say, "*Felidae* eat meat." Other scientists know the zoologist is talking about all kinds of cats—tigers, panthers, and even house cats.

Both domestic cats and wild tigers are part of the group that zoologists call *Felidae*.

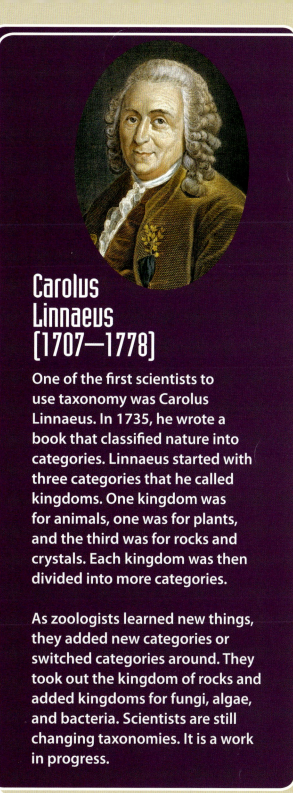

Carolus Linnaeus (1707—1778)

One of the first scientists to use taxonomy was Carolus Linnaeus. In 1735, he wrote a book that classified nature into categories. Linnaeus started with three categories that he called kingdoms. One kingdom was for animals, one was for plants, and the third was for rocks and crystals. Each kingdom was then divided into more categories.

As zoologists learned new things, they added new categories or switched categories around. They took out the kingdom of rocks and added kingdoms for fungi, algae, and bacteria. Scientists are still changing taxonomies. It is a work in progress.

Taxonomy currently has six kingdoms: animal, plant, fungi, protist, archaebacteria, and eubacteria. We will explore the largest of these kingdoms: the kingdom Animalia—the animal kingdom. Animals have three things in common. They are all made up of more than one cell; they don't have cell walls like plant cells do; and they all eat other organisms.

Let's divide the animal kingdom into 17 smaller groups, called phyla. For example, there is a phylum for bugs and one for birds. There are nine phyla for all the various kinds of worms. The phylum you know best is the phylum Chordata, which includes cats, dogs, lizards, birds, and, yes, humans. You are a chordate.

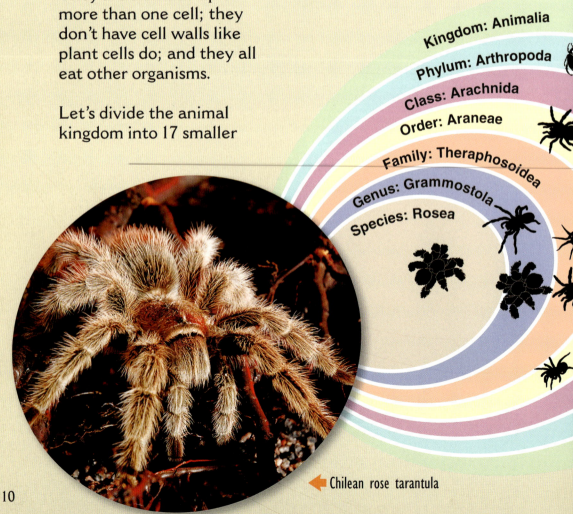

Kingdom: Animalia

Phylum: Arthropoda

Class: Arachnida

Order: Araneae

Family: Theraphosoidea

Genus: Grammostola

Species: Rosea

← Chilean rose tarantula

Taxonomy keeps dividing, spreading out like branches on a tree. Each phylum divides into smaller categories called classes. For example, all birds are in the kingdom Animalia, the phylum Chordata, and the class Aves. Let's branch out further. Classes can be split into orders, and orders divided into families. Within each family is the genus, which can be split into species.

Every living thing fits into a category at each level. Humans are categorized this way: kingdom Animalia, phylum Chordata, class Mammalia, order Primates, family Hominidae, genus *Homo*, and species *Sapiens*. Humans are often referred to just by their genus and species—*Homo sapiens*.

Fun Fact

Can you remember the phrase "Kids Playing Chicken on Freeways Get Smashed"? If you can, remember that the first letter of each word in the phrase is the same as the first letter of the seven levels of taxonomy, in order: kingdom, phylum, class, order, family, genus, species.

Worms, Worms, and More Worms!

There are thousands of kinds of wriggly, burrowing worms in the world. Worms are grouped into nine phyla. Segmented worms—the worms you know best—are in the phylum Annelida.

Worms are very simple animals. They have long, tube-shaped bodies with a mouth on one end and an anus on the other. They don't have brains, and they eat all the time. They feed off single-celled organisms and waste from other animals.

Some worms in the ocean pull water through their bodies. Water goes in through their mouth and out through their anus. Earthworms do the same thing with soil, burrowing through the ground and swallowing soil as they go. They digest whatever they can, and what's left passes out their anus. Earthworms are important to farmers. They churn up the soil as they burrow and eat, which makes the soil better for growing crops.

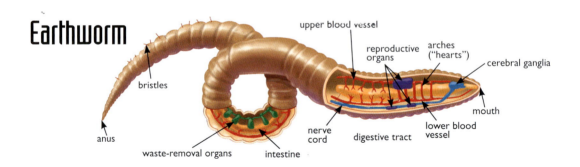

Earthworm

- upper blood vessel
- reproductive organs
- arches ("hearts")
- cerebral ganglia
- mouth
- lower blood vessel
- digestive tract
- nerve cord
- intestine
- waste-removal organs
- anus
- bristles

The Nine Phyla of Worms

Annelida—segmented worms
Nematoda—round worms
Platyhelminthes—flat worms
Hemichordata—sea worms
Sipuncula—peanut worms

Nemertea—ribbon worms
Entoprocta—goblet worms
Phoronida—horseshoe worms
Chaetognatha—arrow worms

The phylum Echinodermata includes ocean animals such as sea urchins, starfish, and sand dollars. The word is Greek for "spiny skin," which is what most echinoderms have.

These animals have either bilateral or radial symmetry. Bilateral symmetry means that one side of the animal is the mirror image of the other side. Humans have bilateral symmetry because their right hand is a mirror image of their left hand, and so on.

Radial symmetry means the animal has many identical parts laid out like the spokes of a wheel. A starfish has radial symmetry: All five arms are identical to each other. In fact, all echinoderms have five-sided radial symmetry.

starfish

Nobody's Perfect

An animal may have symmetry, but that doesn't mean the sides are perfect copies of each other. The right half of your face has the same parts as the left, with eyes, cheekbones, nostrils, ears, and teeth. However, one eye might be just a bit bigger than the other. One ear might be a little higher than the other. The symmetry is only rough. It's not perfect.

What Makes a Mollusk a Mollusk?

Have you ever picked up a slow-moving snail? Have you seen an eight-armed octopus? The snail has a coiled shell with a slimy body. The octopus is wet and quick. They may look very different, but both are mollusks—members of the phylum Mollusca. There is a wide variety of animals in the phylum Mollusca, including clams, oysters, squid, octopuses, and more.

Most mollusks have a hard shell, but some do not. Most have a beaklike radula in their mouth that they use to cut and chew food, but clams do not. Many have one "foot" they use to move around. Squid and octopuses have more than one foot. So why are mollusks grouped together when they don't look alike? It's because they share a common ancestor.

nautilus

◀ Not all mollusks live in the ocean. Snails are mollusks, too.

Zoologists used to group animals together because they look alike. That's called morphological grouping. It's easy to group animals in this way, but it isn't always useful. Scientists often study animals' common ancestors in order to classify them into useful groups called clades.

A clade is a group of animals with a common ancestor. For instance, scientists place ostriches and crocodiles in one clade because they are both descendants of the dinosaur. Mollusks are also a clade. Zoologists studied the cells and organs of living mollusks and concluded that mollusks share a common ancestor. They found that slugs are like snails, except without a shell. They discovered that the arms of octopuses work like the feet of oysters.

Always Changing

Linnaeus and later zoologists observed animals that look alike and used morphological groupings. Many scientists today prefer to group animals in clades according to common ancestors. As scientists learn how various animal species are related, they make changes to the taxonomy.

Spineless but Smart

Some mollusks are grouped into the class Cephalopoda. One cephalopod—the octopus—is thought to be the smartest of all invertebrates, which are animals that don't have a spine. Scientists have seen octopuses get through a maze and solve problems. Some octopuses in zoos have learned to open jars of food.

Spiders, flies, centipedes, and scorpions might all be called bugs. But zoologists call them arthropods, animals in the phylum Arthropoda. Arthropod means "jointed foot," and all arthropods have legs that move. They are also covered with an exoskeleton, a hard, protective outer structure. Your skeleton is inside your body, but theirs is on the outside. Arthropods can move only where their exoskeletons are jointed.

lobster

Arthropods that live in the ocean include lobsters, shrimp, and crabs. These animals with jointed legs share some characteristics with bugs. Look at their pictures side by side and see if you can detect the similarities. That's why they are in the same phylum.

honeybee

All arthropods have many jointed limbs. Some use their limbs as legs and others use them as flippers. Some use them to put food in their mouth. Some centipedes use their limbs to poison their prey. Arthropods' limbs always come in twos—in bilateral symmetry. One side is the same as the other.

centipede

Fun Fact

Have you ever eaten a crab? Most likely it was a soft-shell crab. When a crab gets ready to shed its exoskeleton, the hard shell softens. When crabs are caught during this stage, a chef can prepare the delicacy so the entire crab can be eaten, shell and all.

Arthropods share another trait: segmentation. Their bodies are divided into segments, or parts, that are linked together like the cars of a train. The segments can be very similar or very different. Most of a millipede's similar segments have two legs. A crayfish has several segments: one for walking, one for swimming, and another for sensing the world around it.

barnacle

What Are Barnacles?

Even though they may not look like it, barnacles are animals. These arthropods attach themselves permanently to the outside of hard surfaces such as the bottoms of ships. What looks like a shell is actually the barnacle's exoskeleton. What appear to be leaves or tentacles are jointed limbs. Inside the exoskeleton is a segmented animal. Even though it doesn't move from its position on the hard surface, it still uses its limbs to sweep food into its mouth.

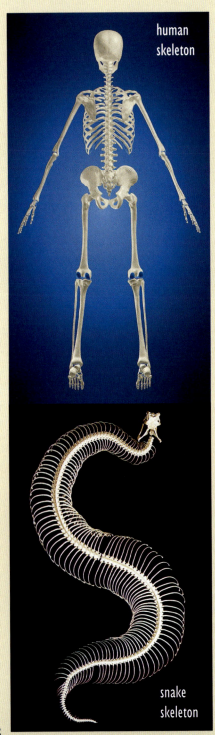

human skeleton

snake skeleton

The last major phylum in the animal kingdom is the one you belong to—phylum Chordata. Reach your hand around to the middle of your back. Can you feel your vertebrae, the bones that make up your backbone? Inside your backbone is your spinal cord, a complex set of nerves that takes messages from your brain to the rest of your body. Because you have a backbone and a spinal cord, you are a member of the phylum Chordata. You are a chordate.

All chordates have or once had a notochord, a stiff but flexible structure inside the embryo. For most chordates, the notochord is replaced with a stronger backbone. Some chordates keep the notochord, and others lose it entirely.

Backbones are very useful. This curved series of vertebrae supports the body. Other bones branch off the backbone to support and protect organs and muscles. Muscles are attached to the backbone to move the whole skeleton. The backbone protects the critical spinal cord and allows an animal to have

dinosaur
skeleton

Chordates Without Backbones

There are two kinds of chordates that are invertebrates—tunicates and lancelets. Tunicates look a lot like seaweed or coral. Lancelets are tiny ocean creatures. Neither animal ever develops a backbone. Tunicate larvae have notochords, but they lose them when they become adults. Lancelets keep their notochords all their lives.

tunicates

a brain that controls the rest of the body. Animals with backbones are called vertebrates. Animals without backbones are invertebrates.

Chordata is a phylum, so it can be split into classes, such as Aves for birds and Sauropsida for reptiles. There are many classes for the thousands of fish in our oceans and lakes. The class Mammalia is for mammals and includes animals such as cats, mice, dogs—and you!

The World of Fish

Do you remember the taxonomy of fish? They are in the kingdom Animalia and the phylum Chordata. All fish have gills, live in water, and are vertebrates with backbones. Scientists group them according to the way they look—morphological grouping. Many fish have not changed over the years. Zoologists call these kinds of fish primitive species because they are a lot like their ancestors.

Fish are first grouped into two superclasses—fish with jaws (Gnathostomata) and fish without (Agnatha). Hagfish and lampreys are Agnatha because they do not have jaws. They are both parasites—they live off of other things. Hagfish enter other fish through the mouth, gills, or anus and eat the fish from the inside out. Lampreys, which have teeth, attach themselves to other fish and suck their blood.

Most of the fish with jaws are classified as Osteichthyes. They have teeth, jaws, and skeletons made of bone. Jaws allow them to eat a variety of foods, including plants and sometimes other animals. Goldfish and salmon belong to this class.

Rows and Rows of Teeth

Sharks have multiple rows of teeth. They lose their teeth constantly and grow new ones to replace them. Over the course of its life, a shark can lose 30,000 teeth.

But when it comes to fish with jaws, the Chondrichthyes class reigns supreme. This group includes rays, skates, and sharks. They have teeth, and their skeletons are made of cartilage. Humans also have cartilage in their bodies; your nose and ears are made of it.

Sarcopterygii may be the strangest of the fish. Members of this class include the huge coelacanth and the much smaller lungfish. Lungfish can breathe air and live in the mud when summers dry up their streams.

Back from the Dead?

Zoologists thought coelacanths were extinct. They could not find any still alive and found only their fossils. Then they found some of these huge fish deep underwater in the Indian Ocean. Coelacanths can grow to about 80 inches (2 meters) long and weigh 175 pounds (80 kilograms). They are related to the lungfish.

lungfish

coelacanth

The Double Life of Amphibians

Frogs, toads, salamanders, newts—you've probably seen them, touched them, and held their wriggly bodies. They are amphibians, the animals that live a double life in water and on land. The word *amphibian* means "two lives." Most frogs are born as tadpoles with no legs. They swim in the water and eat algae. As they grow, they develop legs and lose their tails. Their gills turn into lungs, allowing them to live on land as frogs.

salamander

caecilian

The amphibians that most people think of first are frogs and toads. They make up almost 90 percent of the animals in the phylum Chordata, class Amphibia. The other 10 percent are their relatives.

The class is split into three orders: Anura (frogs and toads), Caudata (salamanders), and

Gymnophiona (caecilians, which look like earthworms, lizards, or snakes but have no scales).

You may wonder why these animals that don't look alike are grouped together. Like mollusks, amphibians are a clade because scientists have identified a common ancestor.

Modern caecilians may be descended from the eocaecilia, an ancient caecilian that had legs like the other amphibians.

common frog

gray tree frog

common toad

Eastern American toad

poison dart frog

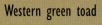
Western green toad

Frog or Toad?

Can you tell the difference between frogs and toads? It's not always easy. Most frogs are green with smooth skin. The common frog is green with spots. The gray tree frog isn't always gray. It changes color to match its surroundings.

Most toads, like the common toad and Eastern American toad, are brown and warty. They blend in well with logs and leaves.

There are many exceptions, though. For example, the poison dart frog is bright red. The Western green toad lives up to its name—it is green from head to foot.

In the end, there is no easy way to tell a frog from a toad based on appearance.

Dinosaurs and Today's Reptiles

Gila monster with eggs

sea turtle

Have you ever watched someone wrestle an alligator? If so, you got a good look at a reptile. Snakes, lizards, turtles, and crocodiles are also reptiles. These animals are in the kingdom Animalia, phylum Chordata, class Sauropsida.

Reptiles have scales, and most of them have four legs. Snakes and worm lizards, however, do not. In fact, they have no legs at all. Most reptiles lay eggs. Their eggs have a special membrane, a thin, skinlike layer that protects the egg. Eggs with this special membrane can be bigger than eggs without it. Bigger eggs mean bigger animals. And bigger animals lay bigger eggs.

As a result, reptiles were the first animals that grew to be really huge. Enormous dinosaurs, also reptiles in the Sauropsida class, once roamed Earth and dominated other animals on the planet. Today dinosaurs are gone, but other reptiles are still around.

crocodile

corn snake

Reptiles can be found on every continent except Antarctica, where it is too cold for reptiles to survive. Reptiles are ectotherms—their bodies do not heat themselves. Instead, their body temperature adjusts by exchanging heat with their surroundings. For example, a reptile lies in the sun to warm up and sits in the shade to cool down. Some reptiles have hearts that can pump backwards, which allows them to move warm blood to cold parts of their bodies. Other reptiles can spread out folds of their skin to soak up more of the sun. There are almost as many ways for an ectotherm to control body heat as there are reptiles.

frilled
lizard →

Built for Flight: Birds

Owls are specially engineered for flight.

Birds are some of the most studied animals on the planet. One reason is because they are very common. Go outside for just a moment, and you will probably see or hear birds. Another reason that zoologists study them is because they are fascinating. Birds can do what many wish they could do—fly!

Birds—vertebrates in the phylum Chordata, class Aves—are built for flight.

Almost every part of a bird's body helps it fly. Birds' skeletons are made of hollow bones, which means they have less mass to raise up into the air. Unlike reptiles, they are endotherms—their own bodies keep them warm. Birds have a lot of energy. Their lungs work twice as hard as yours do, filling up with a good supply of oxygen when they inhale. Instead of a stomach, they have a crop, which stores food, and a gizzard, which

Did You Know?

Birds have no teeth, which means that most of what they eat is swallowed whole. An organ called the gizzard is filled with tiny stones the birds swallow. It grinds the birds' food, making up for their lack of teeth.

ostrich

breaks it down. They need plenty of fuel to have enough energy to beat their wings.

Of course, feather-covered wings are the bird's greatest feature. Feathers are made of long strings of a material called protein, the same kind of protein used by other animals to grow hair, scales, nails, and claws.

Not all birds fly, though. Ostriches, penguins, and kiwi are all flightless. These birds have different feathers and bone structures from flying birds. For instance, the soft, fluffy feathers of the ostrich are very different from the flat, smooth feathers of birds that fly. The ostrich's flat sternum, or breastbone, also makes it impossible for the ostrich to soar into the air.

The last group in the phylum Chordata is class Mammalia. Mammals are vertebrates that have hair or fur and feed milk to their young. Nearly all mammals bear live young. Like birds, they are endotherms that generate their own heat to maintain a constant body temperature. Cows, horses, deer, dogs, dolphin, whales, and so many more are all mammals. You are a mammal, too.

Mammals are some of the most complex organisms on Earth. They have backbones to support complex, sturdy bodies. They have brains that give them behaviors and instincts to help them survive. They can solve problems and adapt to their surroundings. As endotherms, they have a lot of energy. Combine that with their hair or fur, and they are able to live in very cold places.

As complex as mammals are, they can't do everything. Because they breathe air, they can't live on the ocean floor like echinoderms. They have to eat a lot to keep their warm bodies running. Arthropods and amphibians can survive on much less food. Because mammals are so complex, there are more things that can go wrong. Mammals have more diseases than the rest of the animal kingdom.

Mammals are divided into more than 40 orders. Cats, big and small, are in the order Carnivora, which also includes wolves, bears, and seals. The largest order is Rodentia, with more than 2,000 species of mice, rats, squirrels, and chipmunks. Whales and dolphins are in the order Cetecea. The order Primates includes monkeys, apes, and lemurs. Humans are also in the order Primates.

They are separated into their own family (Hominidae), genus (*Homo*), and species (*Sapiens*).

Like all mammals, humans are endotherms: They keep their own bodies warm. They have four limbs, stand upright, and have bilateral symmetry—their left side is a mirror image of their right side. Humans are the most highly developed of the living beings on Earth. The human brain is about three times larger than the largest of all the other animal brains. It is capable of developing new ideas and complex strategies. Humans communicate in complicated languages, solve problems, and experience strong emotions. They have the ability to teach and to learn. Human hands are able to use tools at a higher level than any of the other species. They create great art and music. Working together, humans can create advanced civilizations.

The animal kingdom is enormous and diverse. The incredible varieties make the world an exciting, interesting place. How fortunate we humans are to be a part of it!

Monotremes

Monotremes (order Monotrema) are the only mammals that lay eggs instead of giving birth to live young. The echidna and the platypus are monotremes. When the platypus was first discovered in the late 1700s, a dead, stuffed platypus was sent to Great Britain. British scientists thought the animal was a fake. They tried to find the stitches that connected the "beaver" tail and the "duck" bill to the furry body.

platypus

"Bald" Whales

Like all other mammals, whales have hair. They are born with a little fuzz on their skin. But as they grow older, they lose their fuzz. For the rest of their lives, they are "bald," or have no hair. But they did when they were born!

Bacterial Growth in Saliva

Whose mouth is cleaner—a dog's or a human's? You can find out by experimenting with saliva. If you test the saliva from a dog and from a human, you can find out which one grows more bacteria faster. In addition to the materials, you'll need a friendly dog for this activity. Be sure to wash your hands between each step, and carefully clean or discard your materials when you are finished.

Materials

- 8 sterile nutrient agar petri dishes (can be ordered online)
- marker
- labels
- cotton swabs
- pencil and chart for recording observations
- camera for taking photos (digital or Polaroid preferred)

Procedure

1   Check to be sure your petri dishes are clean. Place a label on the lid of each dish. Number each dish (1–8). Then label dishes 1–4 with the word *DOG*; label dishes 5–8 with the word *HUMAN*.

2 In the morning, before breakfast, wash your hands with soap. Collect a saliva sample from your dog. Using a sterile cotton swab, swipe the inside of your dog's mouth to collect some saliva. Make sure the saliva is not taken from outside the dog's mouth. (On the outside, the saliva could pick up bacteria from the dog's coat, your carpet, or other places)

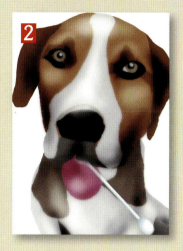

3 Open dish 1 DOG. Gently wipe the saliva-coated swab across the agar. Close the dish with its labeled lid. Set it in a safe place at room temperature. Take a picture of the dish.

4 Wash your hands with soap. Using a new cotton swab, swipe the inside of your own mouth to collect some saliva. Open dish 5 HUMAN. Gently wipe the saliva-coated swab across the agar. Close the dish with its labeled lid. Set it in a safe place at room temperature. Take a picture of the dish.

6 Gather saliva by repeating procedures 2–5 three more times—that evening, the next morning, and the next evening. Use new dishes each time and chart your activities.

7 The day after each sample is collected, chart any changes you observe in each dish. Rate the bacteria growth you see in each dish. You may use the words *none*, *a little*, or *a lot*. Take pictures each day.

8 After five days of recording your observations for each sample, print your pictures. Label the pictures with the dish number as well as the time and date of the photograph.

9 Now draw your conclusions. Which dishes grew bacteria faster? Whose mouth is cleaner—a dog's or a human's?

10 Summarize your findings.

Francis Maitland Balfour (1851–1882)
British zoologist who made several suggestions for animal classification, including that animals with backbones be classed as Chordata, a term that is still used today

Caspar Bauhin (1560–1624)
Swiss botanist who developed the use of genus and species names for classification

Pierre Belon (1517–1564)
French naturalist who determined that many species had skeletal similarities; classified more than 200 species and compared the bones of humans and birds

Charles Robert Darwin (1809–1882)
British naturalist who revolutionized biology with his theory of evolution through the process of natural selection

Theodore Nicholas Gill (1837–1914)
American ichthyologist (scientist who studies fish) and outstanding taxonomist of his time; had a major influence on the field of ichthyology

Carolus Linnaeus (1707–1778)
Swedish naturalist who introduced certain classifications of organisms that are still in use today

John Ray (1628–1705)
British naturalist and taxonomist who first proposed the concept of species; helped to lay the groundwork for classification systems

Sir Charles Wyville Thomson (1830–1882)
British marine biologist who determined that life exists deep in the oceans

Alexander Wilson (1706–1813)
British-born American who was the founder of ornithology (the study of birds) in the United States; drew and wrote about birds and noted 48 species previously unknown in the United States

Glossary

amphibians—animals belonging to the class Amphibia that are at home both on land and in the water

ancestor—organism from which another organism descended

Animalia—animal kingdom

anus—opening through which solid waste leaves the body

arthropods—animals belonging to the phylum Arthropoda that have an exoskeleton and jointed limbs with bilateral symmetry

bilateral symmetry— kind of symmetry in which one side is the mirror image of the other

cartilage—material softer than bone, found in animal skeletons

cell—smallest unit of living things

chordates—animals belonging to the phylum Chordata, who at some stage have developed a notochord

clade—group of animals descended from a common ancestor

class—the third level of taxonomy, between phylum and order

echinoderm—marine animal with five-sided radial symmetry (starfish and sand dollars)

ectotherms—animals that rely on their surroundings to maintain their heat

embryo—animal organism in its early stages of development

endotherms—animals that can produce their own heat

exoskeleton—hard outer structure of an animal that provides protection or support

extinct—no longer existing; having no living members of a species

family—the fifth level of taxonomy, between order and genus

genus—the sixth level of taxonomy, between family and species

invertebrates—animals without a backbone

kingdom—the first level of taxonomy that is divided into phyla

membrane—skinlike layer that separates living tissues

mollusk—diverse group of usually marine animals that belong to the phylum Mollusca and share a common ancestor

morphological grouping—organized by form and structure

notochord—flexible rodlike structure that supports the body of some lower chordates or forms a spinal column in higher chordates

order—the fourth level of taxonomy, between class and family

phylum (phyla)—the second level of taxonomy, between kingdom and class

primitive—animal that has not changed much from its ancestor

protein—tough material animals use to grow body features

radial symmetry—kind of symmetry in which many identical parts are laid out like the spokes of a wheel

radula—beaklike organ that many mollusks use to eat

reptiles—animals belonging to the class Sauropsida that are ectotherms and are covered in scales rather than fur or feathers

segmented—separated into different parts of the whole

species—the seventh and lowest level of taxonomy; a specific kind of animal

symmetry—way an organism is structured; can be bilateral (two mirrored sides) or radial (like spokes on a wheel)

taxonomy—classification of organisms into an ordered system

vertebrae—bones that make up a backbone and surround and protect the spinal cord

vertebrate—animal with a backbone

zoologists—scientists who study animal life

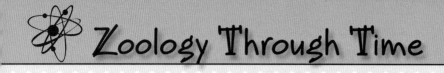

350 B.C.	Aristotle groups 500 known species of animals into eight classes
100 B.C.	First zoo, the Park of Intelligence, is founded in China
50 A.D.	Pliny the Elder writes *Naturalis Historia* that describes what was known about zoology at that time
1517	Naturalist Pierre Belon is first to note similarities between certain bones from fish and mammals
1551	Swiss naturalist Konrad von Gesner writes a book that begins the science of zoology
1599	First serious book on zoology is written by Ulisse Aldrovani
1623	Caspar Bauhin develops the use of the names genus and species
1693	John Ray writes a book that includes the first important classification of animals
1734	*The History of Insects* by René de Réaumur lays the foundation for entomology, the study of insects
1735	Carolus Linnaeus introduces a classification of organisms still in use today
1761	First veterinary school is founded in Lyons, France
1795	George Cuvier develops a method of classifying mammals
1803	First wild bird banding studies are conducted in America by John Otto

1813	The term *taxonomy* is introduced by Augustin de Candolle
1822	Jean Lamarck distinguishes between invertebrates and vertebrates
1858	Three communications to the Linnean Society describe the theory of evolution by natural selection, including reports from Charles Darwin and Alfred Wallace
1859	Charles Darwin publishes his *On the Origin of Species,* detailing natural selection and evolution
1901	Hugo De Vries determines that changes in a species occur in jumps, which he calls mutations
1953	A supposedly extinct fish, the coelacanth, turns out to be common around the Comoro Islands off the African coast
1960	Kenneth Norris and John Prescott find that bottlenose dolphins use echolocation (similar to sonar) to locate objects in water
1988	First patent is issued for a vertebrate, a mouse developed by genetic engineering at Harvard Medical School
1992	The oldest organism known to exist is discovered in Michigan; it is a 1,500-year-old fungus covering 30 acres (12 hectares) underground
2008	A University of California, Santa Barbara, study of island ecosystems suggests that wildlife diversity is increasing, not decreasing

Stonehouse, Bernard, and Esther Bertram. *How Animals Live: The Amazing World of Animals in the Wild*. New York: Scholastic, 2004.

Gilpin, Daniel. *Starfish, Urchins & Other Echinoderms*. Minneapolis: Compass Point Books, 2006.

McGhee, Karen, and George McKay. *Encyclopedia of Animals*. Washington, D.C.: National Geographic Children's Books, 2007.

Mound, Laurence. *Insect*. New York: DK Publishing, 2007.

Parker, Steve. *Bats, Blue Whales & Other Mammals*. Minneapolis: Compass Point Books, 2005.

On the Web

For more information on this topic, use FactHound.

1. Go to *www.facthound.com*
2. Choose your grade level.
3. Begin your search.

This book's ID number is 9780756540579

FactHound will find the best sites for you.

Index

Joshua BishopRoby

Joshua BishopRoby is a book author and publisher who also designs and publishes role-playing games. He began his career in high school when he founded the school's literary magazine. BishopRoby has an interest and wide breadth of knowledge in many subjects, including science. He is formerly a secondary level teacher. He makes his home in Southern California.

Image Credits